Best Knock-Knock Book Ever

Charles Keller

Illustrated by Jeff Sinclair

Sterling Publishing Co., Inc.
New York

To Gabriel and Bowen

I would like to acknowledge the help of Stephen Blance, Marcus Bocchino, Rhoda Crispell, and Brenda Gordon.

Library of Congress Cataloging-in-Publication Data

Keller, Charles.
    Best knock-knock book ever / Charles Keller ; illustrated by Jeff Sinclair.
      p.   cm.
    Includes index.
    Summary: An alphabetically arranged collection of knock-knock jokes playing on names, initials, and phrases.
    ISBN 0-8069-6513-4
    1. Knock-knock jokes. [1. Knock-knock jokes. 2. Jokes.] I. Sinclair, Jeff, ill. II. Title.
    PN623.1K425 2000
    818'.5402–dc21

                                   99-049402

20 19 18 17 16

First paperback edition published in 2001 by
Sterling Publishing Co., Inc.
387 Park Avenue South, New York, NY 10016
© 2000 by Charles Keller
Distributed in Canada by Sterling Publishing
c/o Canadian Manda Group, 165 Dufferin Street,
Toronto, Ontario, Canada M6K 3H6
Distributed in Great Britain and Europe by Chris Lloyd at Orca Book
Services, Stanley House, Fleets Lane, Poole BH15 3AJ, England
Distributed in Australia by Capricorn Link (Australia) Pty. Ltd.
P.O. Box 704, Windsor, NSW 2756, Australia

Sterling ISBN-13: 978-0-8069-6529-1
        ISBN-10: 0-8069-6529-0

For information about custom editions, special sales, premium and corporate purchases, please contact Sterling Special Sales Department at 800-805-5489 or specialsales@sterlingpub.com.

Contents

Knock-knock.
Who's there?
Aaron.
Aaron who?
Aaron all the way home.

Knock-knock.
Who's there?
Abbot.
Abbot who?
Abbot time we eat, isn't it?

Knock-knock.
Who's there?
Abe Lincoln.
Abe Lincoln who?
Abe Lincoln break in the strongest chain.

Knock-knock.
  Who's there?
A.C.
  A.C. who?
A.C. come and A.C. go.

Knock-knock.
  Who's there?
Acme.
  Acme who?
If you acme I'll tell you.

Knock-knock.
  Who's there?
Adam.
  Adam who?
Adam up and give me the bill.

Knock-knock.
  Who's there?
Adore.
  Adore who?
Adore is between us.

Knock-knock.
  Who's there?
A.E.
  A.E. who?
A.E. I owe you.

Knock-knock.
Who's there?
Aikido.
Aikido who?
Aikido you not.

Knock-knock.
Who's there?
Alaska.
Alaska who?
Alaska and you ask him.

Knock-knock.
Who's there?
Alex.
Alex who?
Alex plain later.

Knock-knock.
  Who's there?
Alfreda.
  Alfreda who?
Alfreda the dark.

Knock-knock.
  Who's there?
Amarillo.
  Amarillo who?
Amarillo-fashioned girl.

Knock-knock.
  Who's there?
Amen.
  Amen who?
Amen hot water again.

Knock-knock.
  Who's there?
Amnesia.
  Amnesia who?
Oh, you got it too.

Knock-knock.
  Who's there?
Andy.
  Andy who?
Andy all lived happily ever after.

Knock-knock.
Who's there?
Andy.
Andy who?
Andy music goes on and on.

Knock-knock.
Who's there?
Anita.
Anita who?
Anita you like Anita hole in the head.

Knock-knock.
Who's there?
Anita.
Anita who?
Anita ride into town.

Knock-knock.
  Who's there?
Anvil.
  Anvil who?
Anvil you be coming too?

Knock-knock.
  Who's there?
Apricot.
  Apricot who?
Apricot my key, open up.

Knock-knock.
  Who's there?
A quorum.
  A quorum who?
A quorum is where I keep my fish.

Knock-knock.
  Who's there?
Arizona.
  Arizona who?
Arizona room for one of us in this town.

Knock-knock.
  Who's there?
Arm.
  Arm who?
Arm always chasing rainbows.

Knock-knock.
Who's there?
Armstrong.
Armstrong who?
Armstrong as an ox.

Knock-knock.
Who's there?
Ash.
Ash who?
Bless you.

Knock-knock.
Who's there?
Asparagus.
Asparagus who?
Asparagus the argument, we don't want to hear it.

Knock-knock.
  Who's there?
Astor.
  Astor who?
Astor what her name is.

Knock-knock.
  Who's there?
Atlas.
  Atlas who?
Atlas I'm here.

Knock-knock.
  Who's there?
Avenue.
  Avenue who?
Avenue heard this joke before?

Knock-knock.
Who's there?
Babylon.
Babylon who?
Babylon if you must.

Knock-knock.
Who's there?
Bella.
Bella who?
Bella the ball.

Knock-knock.
Who's there?
Ben and Don.
Ben and Don who?
Ben there, Don that.

13

Knock-knock.
Who's there?
Bernie D.
Bernie D who?
Bernie D candles at both ends.

Knock-knock.
Who's there?
Bertha.
Bertha who?
Bertha the blues.

Knock-knock.
Who's there:
Bette.
Bette who?
Bette you can't guess my name.

Knock-knock.
Who's there?
Blank.
Blank who?
You're welcome.

Knock-knock.
Who's there?
Blast.
Blast who?
Blast, but not least.

Knock-knock.
  Who's there?
Bolivia.
  Bolivia who?
Bolivia me!

Knock-knock.
  Who's there?
Booty.
  Booty who?
Booty is only skin deep.

Knock-knock.
  Who's there?
Button.
  Button who?
Button into what's not your business.

Knock-knock.
Who's there?
Cameron.
Cameron who?
Cameron over here.

Knock-knock.
Who's there?
Candace.
Candace who.
Candace door be opened?

Knock-knock.
Who's there?
Canoe.
Canoe who?
Canoe help me with my homework?

Knock-knock.
Who's there?
Carlo.
Carlo who?
Carlo on gas.

Knock-knock.
Who's there?
Casino.
Casino who?
Casino evil.

Knock-knock.
Who's there?
Castanet.
Castanet who?
Castanet in the water to catch fish.

Knock-knock.
Who's there?
C.D.
C.D. who?
C.D. forest for the trees.

Knock-knock.
Who's there?
Censure.
Censure who?
Censure letters by first class mail.

Knock-knock.
Who's there?
Cereal.
Cereal who?
Cereal McCoy.

Knock-knock.
Who's there?
Chantelle.
Chantelle who?
Chantelle you anything.

Knock-knock.
Who's there?
Checker.
Checker who?
Checker out.

Knock-knock.
Who's there?
Cheese.
Cheese who?
Cheese funny that way.

Knock-knock.
Who's there?
Cindy.
Cindy who?
Cindy movie, read the book.

Knock-knock.
Who's there?
Clancy.
Clancy who?
Clancy where I'm going.

Knock-knock.
Who's there?
Coma.
Coma who?
Coma your hair.

Knock-knock.
Who's there?
Conan.
Conan who?
Conan the cob.

Knock-knock.
 Who's there?
Conscience stricken.
 Conscience stricken who?
Don't conscience stricken before they hatch.

Knock-knock.
 Who's there?
Cows.
 Cows who?
No, cows moo.

Knock-knock.
 Who's there?
Crate.
 Crate who?
Crate to be here.

Knock-knock.
Who's there?
Crepes.
Crepes who?
Crepes of Wrath.

Knock-knock.
Who's there?
Crimea.
Crimea who?
"Crimea River."

Knock-knock.
Who's there?
Cybil.
Cybil who?
Cybil War.

Knock-knock.
Who's there?
Cypress.
Cypress who?
Cypress your suit.

Knock-knock.
Who's there?
Czar.
Czar who?
Czar she blows!

Knock-knock.
Who's there?
Dakota.
Dakota who?
Dakota fits fine, the pants are too long.

Knock-knock.
Who's there?
Darby.
Darby who?
Darby stung me.

Knock-knock.
Who's there?
Darrel.
Darrel who?
Darrel never be another you.

Knock-knock.
Who's there?
Darwin.
Darwin who?
Darwin young man on the flying trapeze.

Knock-knock.
Who's there?
Dawn.
Dawn who?
Dawn bite off more than you can chew.

Knock-knock.
Who's there?
Debt.
Debt who?
Debt men tell no tales.

Knock-knock.
Who's there?
Dee.
Dee who?
Dee joke's on me.

Knock-knock.
Who's there?
Defense.
Defense who?
Defense keeps the dog in.

Knock-knock.
Who's there?
Demure.
Demure who?
Demure you get, Demure you want.

Knock-knock.
Who's there?
Demure.
Demure who?
Demure the merrier.

Knock-knock.
Who's there?
Dennis.
Dennis who?
Dennis this rain going to stop?

Knock-knock.
Who's there?
Denver.
Denver who?
Denver in the world are we?

Knock-knock.
Who's there?
Depend.
Depend who?
Depend is mightier than the sword.

Knock-knock.
Who's there?
Derby.
Derby who?
Derby ghosts in that haunted house.

Knock-knock.
Who's there?
Diesel.
Diesel who?
Diesel be your last chance.

Knock-knock.
Who's there?
Dina.
Dina who?
Dina at eight.

Knock-knock.
Who's there?
Dinosaur.
Dinosaur who?
Dinosaur at you—you burnt the toast.

Knock-knock.
Who's there?
Divide.
Divide who?
Divide world of sports.

Knock-knock.
Who's there?
Dobie.
Dobie who?
Dobie cruel to animals.

Knock-knock.
  Who's there?
Dole.
  Dole who?
Dole truth and nothing but the truth.

Knock-knock.
  Who's there?
Don and Greta.
  Don and Greta who?
Don and Greta round much any more.

Knock-knock.
  Who's there?
Don.
  Don who?
Don want to tell you my name.

Knock-knock.
  Who's there?
Doughnut.
  Doughnut who?
Doughnut thing till you hear from me.

Knock-knock.
  Who's there?
Duane.
  Duane who?
Duane the bathtub, rubber ducky drowning.

Knock-knock.
  Who's there?
Duncan.
  Duncan who?
Duncan your doughnut again?

Knock-knock.
  Who's there?
Dustin.
  Dustin who?
Dustin furniture with polish.

Knock-knock.
  Who's there?
Dwight.
  Dwight who?
Dwight as rain.

Knock-knock.
Who's there?
Eamon.
Eamon who?
Eamon the mood for love.

Knock-knock.
Who's there?
Eben.
Eben who?
Eben a good girl.

Knock-knock.
Who's there?
Eddy.
Eddy who?
Eddy body got a tissue? I've got a cold.

Knock-knock.
Who's there?
Effie.
Effie who?
"Effie Thing's Coming Up Roses."

Knock-knock.
Who's there?
Eggs.
Eggs who?
Eggs marks the spot.

Knock-knock.
Who's there?
Egos.
Egos who?
Egos wherever he wants to.

Knock-knock.
Who's there?
Eisenhower.
Eisenhower who?
Eisenhower late for school.

Knock-knock.
Who's there?
Elise.
Elise who?
Elise signed by a tenant.

Knock-knock.
Who's there?
Eliza.
Eliza who?
Eliza lot, so watch your step.

Knock-knock.
Who's there?
Ella Vance.
Ella Vance who?
Ella Vance never forget.

Knock-knock.
Who's there?
Erie.
Erie who?
Erie is, right on time.

31

Knock-knock.
Who's there?
Eschew.
Eschew who?
Eschew goes on your foot.

Knock-knock.
Who's there?
Estelle.
Estelle who?
Estelle waiting for you to open the door.

Knock-knock.
Who's there?
Etch.
Etch who?
Bless you.

Knock-knock.
Who's there?
Ethan.
Ethan who?
Ethan everything in sight.

Knock-knock.
Who's there?
Eugenes.
Eugenes who?
Eugenes need washing.

Knock-knock.
   Who's there?
Europa.
   Europa who?
Europa steer and I'll watch.

Knock-knock.
   Who's there?
Ewer.
   Ewer who?
Ewer getting sleepy.

Knock-knock.
   Who's there?
Eyelet.
   Eyelet who?
Eyelet you in.

Knock-knock.
Who's there?
Falsetto.
Falsetto who?
Falsetto teeth.

Knock-knock.
Who's there?
Fender.
Fender who?
Fender moon comes over the mountain.

Knock-knock.
Who's there?
Ferdinand.
Ferdinand who?
Ferdinand is worth two in the bush.

34

Knock-knock.
Who's there?
Flea.
Flea who?
"Flea, fie, foh, fum."

Knock-knock.
Who's there?
Florist.
Florist who?
Florist the opposite of ceiling.

Knock-knock.
Who's there?
Flossie.
Flossie who?
Flossie your teeth.

Knock-knock.
Who's there?
Forest.
Forest who?
Forest the eye can see.

Knock-knock.
Who's there?
Fortification.
Fortification who?
Fortification I go to the seashore.

Knock-knock.
Who's there?
Francine.
Francine who?
Francine it all.

Knock-knock.
Who's there?
Frieda.
Frieda who?
"Who's a Frieda the Big Bad Wolf?"

Knock-knock.
Who's there?
Fritz.
Fritz who?
"Fritz a Wonderful Life."

Knock-knock.
  Who's there?
Garter.
  Garter who?
Garter date with an angel.

Knock-knock.
  Who's there?
Gary.
  Gary who?
Gary the package for me.

Knock-knock.
  Who's there?
Gas.
  Gas who?
"Gas Who's Coming to Dinner."

Knock-knock.
  Who's there?
G.I.
  G.I. who?
G.I. don't know.

Knock-knock.
  Who's there?
Gladwin.
  Gladwin who?
Gladwin you're leaving.

Knock-knock.
  Who's there?
Glove.
  Glove who?
"Glove is a Many-Splendored Thing."

Knock-knock.
  Who's there?
Goatee.
  Goatee who?
Goatee off—the other golfers are waiting.

Knock-knock.
  Who's there?
Goosie.
  Goosie who?
Goosie who's at the door.

Knock-knock.
Who's there?
Gouda.
Gouda who?
Gouda see you again.

Knock-knock.
Who's there?
Gruesome.
Gruesome who?
Gruesome tomatoes in my garden.

Knock-knock.
Who's there?
Gwen.
Gwen who?
Gwen will I see you again?

Knock-knock.
Who's there?
Hair combs.
Hair combs who?
Hair combs the bride.

Knock-knock.
Who's there?
Half.
Half who?
Half I got a girl for you.

Knock-knock.
Who's there?
Hall.
Hall who?
"Hall the king's horses and hall the king's men."

Knock-knock.
  Who's there?
Hallow.
  Hallow who?
Hallow down there.

Knock-knock.
  Who's there?
Hannibal.
  Hannibal who?
Hannibal in a china shop.

Knock-knock.
  Who's there?
Hans.
  Hans who?
Hans off my computer.

Knock-knock.
  Who's there?
Harpy.
  Harpy who?
Harpy to see you again.

Knock-knock.
  Who's there?
Harris.
  Harris who?
"Harris looking at you, kid."

Knock-knock.
Who's there?
Harry.
Harry who?
Harry up, I'm starving.

Knock-knock.
Who's there?
Harvey.
Harvey who?
Harvey going to stop meeting like this?

Knock-knock.
Who's there?
Harvey Gotti.
Harvey Gotti who?
Harvey Gotti wait here all night?

Knock-knock.
Who's there?
Heaven.
Heaven who?
Heaven you heard enough knock-knock jokes?

Knock-knock.
Who's there?
Hector.
Hector who?
"Hector halls with boughs of holly."

Knock-knock.
  Who's there?
Hedda.
  Hedda who?
Hedda off at the pass.

Knock-knock.
  Who's there?
Highway cop.
  Highway cop who?
Highway cop at seven every morning.

Knock-knock.
  Who's there?
Hippie.
  Hippie who?
Hippie birthday to you.

Knock-knock.
Who's there?
Honor.
Honor who?
"Honor clear day you can see forever."

Knock-knock.
Who's there?
Hoover.
Hoover who?
Hoover you expecting?

Knock-knock.
Who's there?
Horace.
Horace who?
Horace and buggy.

Knock-knock.
Who's there?
House.
House who?
House business?

Knock-knock.
Who's there?
Hugh.
Hugh who?
Hugh who yourself.

Knock-knock.
Who's there?
Humphrey.
Humphrey who?
Humphrey ever blowing bubbles.

Knock-knock.
Who's there?
Hunger.
Hunger who?
Hunger wash out to dry.

Knock-knock.
Who's there?
Huron.
Huron who?
Huron time for once.

Knock-knock.
Who's there?
Ice water.
Ice water who?
Ice water fly with my fly swatter.

Knock-knock.
Who's there?
Ida.
Ida who?
Ida who potato.

Knock-knock.
Who's there?
Imus.
Imus who?
Imus get in out of the rain.

Knock-knock.
Who's there?
India.
India who?
India cool, cool of the evening.

Knock-knock.
Who's there?
Indy.
Indy who?
Indy mood.

Knock-knock.
Who's there?
Iraq.
Iraq who?
Iraq my brain but couldn't get the answer.

Knock-knock.
Who's there?
Irish.
Irish who?
Irish upon a star.

Knock-knock.
  Who's there?
Irma.
  Irma who?
Irma going to sit right down and write myself a
  letter.

Knock-knock.
  Who's there?
Iron.
  Iron who?
Iron joy being a girl.

Knock-knock.
  Who's there?
Isidore.
  Isidore who?
Isidore unlocked?

Knock-knock.
   Who's there?
Israel.
   Israel who?
Israel or fake?

Knock-knock.
   Who's there?
Issue.
   Issue who?
Issue ready to go?

Knock-knock.
   Who's there?
Itzhak.
   Itzhak who?
"Itzhak small world after all."

Knock-knock.
   Who's there?
Ivan.
   Ivan who?
Ivan, you lose.

Knock-knock.
Who's there?
Jackson.
Jackson who?
Jackson the box.

Knock-knock.
Who's there?
Jaws.
Jaws who?
Jaws till the well runs dry.

Knock-knock.
Who's there?
Jenny.
Jenny who?
Jenny a hearing aid? I've been knocking for five
    minutes.

Knock-knock.
Who's there?
Jenny.
Jenny who?
Jenny body home?

Knock-knock.
Who's there?
Jess.
Jess who?
Jess in time.

Knock-knock.
Who's there?
Jewel.
Jewel who?
Jewel be sorry.

Knock-knock.
Who's there?
Jimmy.
Jimmy who?
Jimmy liberty or Jimmy death.

Knock-knock.
Who's there?
Josie.
Josie who?
Josie who's at the door.

Knock-knock.
Who's there?
Jules.
Jules who?
Jules are in the safe.

Knock-knock.
Who's there?
Juliet.
Juliet who?
Juliet the cat out of the bag.

Knock-knock.
Who's there?
Junior.
Junior who?
Junior flowers will come up.

Knock-knock.
Who's there?
Juno.
Juno who?
I don't know, Juno?

Knock-knock.
Who's there?
Jupiter.
Jupiter who?
Jupiter note on my door?

Knock-knock.
Who's there?
Justice.
Justice who?
Justice I got home the phone rang.

Knock-knock.
Who's there?
Justin.
Justin who?
"Justin time, I found you Justin time."

Knock-knock.
Who's there?
Karaoke.
Karaoke who?
Karaoke or not okay?

Knock-knock.
Who's there?
Katmandu.
Katmandu who?
Katmandu what Catwoman wants.

Knock-knock.
Who's there?
Kermit.
Kermit who?
Kermit me to introduce myself.

Knock-knock.
Who's there?
Ketchup.
Ketchup who?
Ketchup with her before she gets away.

Knock-knock.
Who's there?
Kip.
Kip who?
Kip your sunny side up.

Knock-knock.
Who's there?
Knoxville.
Knoxville who?
Knoxville get you an answer if you wait long enough.

Knock-knock.
Who's there?
Koala-T.
Koala-T who?
Koala-T knock-knocks are hard to find.

Knock-knock.
Who's there?
Kokomo.
Kokomo who?
Kokomo food—I'm hungry.

Knock-knock.
Who's there?
Land.
Land who?
It's "land-ho," not "land who."

Knock-knock.
Who's there?
Levin.
Levin who?
"Levin on a jet plane."

Knock-knock.
Who's there?
Leopold.
Leopold who?
Leopold the class and everyone wants a new teacher.

Knock-knock.
Who's there?
Letter.
Letter who?
Letter smile be your umbrella.

Knock-knock.
Who's there?
Lice.
Lice who?
Lice out by ten o'clock.

Knock-knock.
Who's there?
Lilac.
Lilac who?
Lilac that and you'll get punished.

Knock-knock.
Who's there?
Liv.
Liv who?
Liv no stone unturned.

Knock-knock.
Who's there?
Liver.
Liver who?
Liver round here?

Knock-knock.
Who's there?
Macon.
Macon who?
"Macon a list, checking it twice."

Knock-knock.
Who's there?
Macon.
Macon who?
Macon whoopie.

Knock-knock.
Who's there?
Major.
Major who?
Major bed, now lie in it.

Knock-knock.
Who's there?
Mandalay.
Mandalay who?
Mandalay the kitchen tiles.

Knock-knock.
Who's there?
Massachusetts.
Massachusetts who?
Massachusetts is what you hear when a train blows
its whistle.

Knock-knock.
Who's there?
Mayonnaise.
Mayonnaise who?
"Mayonnaise be merry and bright..."

Knock-knock.
Who's there?
Melissa.
Melissa who?
Melissa longer than your list.

Knock-knock.
Who's there?
Me.
Me who?
Meow.

Knock-knock.
Who's there?
Menu.
Menu who?
Menu stay here, women over there.

Knock-knock.
Who's there?
Michigan.
Michigan who?
"Michigan," said the batter after the third strike.

Knock-knock.
Who's there?
Midas.
Midas who?
Midas well open up, I'm not going away.

Knock-knock.
Who's there?
Mira.
Mira who?
Mira, Mira, on the wall.

Knock-knock.
Who's there?
Monet.
Monet who?
Monet burns a hole in my pocket.

Knock-knock.
Who's there?
Moose.
Moose who?
Moose beautiful girl in the world.

Knock-knock.
Who's there?
Mustard.
Mustard who?
Mustard been a beautiful baby.

Knock-knock.
Who's there?
Nathan.
Nathan who?
Nathan to lose.

Knock-knock.
Who's there?
Nestor.
Nestor who?
Nestor lives my neighbor.

Knock-knock.
Who's there?
Newark.
Newark who?
Newark for Noah.

Knock-knock.
  Who's there?
Newark.
  Newark who?
Newark keeps piling up.

Knock-knock.
  Who's there?
Noggin.
  Noggin who?
Noggin at your door.

Knock-knock.
  Who's there?
Notify.
  Notify who?
Notify can help it.

Knock-knock.
  Who's there?
Nova.
  Nova who?
Nova look back.

Knock-knock.
 Who's there?
O. A.
 O. A. who?
"O. A. down South in Dixie."

Knock-knock.
 Who's there?
Occult.
 Occult who?
Occult in my nose.

Knock-knock.
 Who's there?
Ocelot.
 Ocelot who?
Ocelot of money for that.

Knock-knock.
  Who's there?
Ohio.
  Ohio who?
Ohio than the highest mountain.

Knock-knock.
  Who's there?
Oil well.
  Oil well who?
Oil well that ends well.

Knock-knock.
  Who's there?
Oklahoma.
  Oklahoma who?
Oklahoma and wash your face.

Knock-knock.
  Who's there?
Olaf.
  Olaf who?
"Olaf My Heart in San Francisco."

Knock-knock.
  Who's there?
One door.
  One door who?
One door where you are tonight.

Knock-knock.
Who's there?
Opel.
Opel who?
Opel of mine.

Knock-knock.
Who's there?
Orange shoe.
Orange shoe who?
Orange shoe going to let me in?

Knock-knock.
Who's there?
Oregon.
Oregon who?
Oregon and I'm not coming back.

Knock-knock.
Who's there?
Orson.
Orson who?
Orson buggy—want a ride?

Knock-knock.
Who's there?
Osborne.
Osborne who?
Osborne in the hospital.

Knock-knock.
  Who's there?
Osgood.
  Osgood who?
Osgood as it gets.

Knock-knock.
  Who's there?
Oslo.
  Oslo who?
Oslo down, you're going too fast.

Knock-knock.
  Who's there?
Oswego.
  Oswego who?
"Oswego into the wild blue yonder."

Knock-knock.
  Who's there?
Otter.
  Otter who?
Otter apologize for these bad jokes.

Knock-knock.
  Who's there?
O. Verdi.
  O. Verdi who?
"O. Verdi Rainbow."

Knock-knock.
  Who's there?
Owls.
  Owls who?
You got it right this time.

Knock-knock.
Who's there?
Paddy.
Paddy who?
Paddy your own canoe.

Knock-knock.
Who's there?
Pakistan.
Pakistan who?
Pakistan lunch. He's working late.

Knock-knock.
Who's there?
Pasadena.
Pasadena who?
Stop when you Pasadena—I'm hungry.

Knock-knock.
Who's there?
Pasteurize.
Pasteurize who?
Pasteurize and over the gums, look out stomach,
here it comes.

Knock-knock.
Who's there?
Patella.
Patella who?
Patella story before bedtime.

Knock-knock.
Who's there?
Paula.
Paula who?
Paula few strings for me.

Knock-knock.
Who's there?
Pawtucket.
Pawtucket who?
I had a dollar, but Pawtucket.

Knock-knock.
Who's there?
Pay cents.
Pay cents who?
Pay cents is a virtue.

Knock-knock.
Who's there?
Peekaboo.
Peekaboo who?
Peekaboo live in glass houses shouldn't throw stones.

Knock-knock.
Who's there?
Peking.
Peking who?
Peking is not allowed.

Knock-knock.
Who's there?
Pembroke.
Pembroke who?
Pembroke, can I use yours?

Knock-knock.
Who's there?
Picture.
Picture who?
Picture favorite flowers.

Knock-knock.
Who's there?
Plate.
Plate who?
"Plate again, Sam."

Knock-knock.
Who's there?
Poker.
Poker who?
Poker Hontas.

Knock-knock.
Who's there?
Poland.
Poland who?
Poland or rich country?

Knock-knock.
Who's there?
Quaint.
Quaint who?
"Quaint nothing but a hound dog."

Knock-knock.
Who's there?
Quake.
Quake who?
Quake up, you sleepyhead.

Knock-knock.
Who's there?
Que Sarah.
Que Sarah who?
"Que Sarah, Sarah; whatever will be, will be."

Knock-knock.
Who's there?
Radio.
Radio who?
Radio not, here I come.

Knock-knock.
Who's there?
Randy and Vanna.
Randy and Vanna who?
Randy race and Vanna medal.

Knock-knock.
Who's there?
Raptor.
Raptor who?
Raptor presents before Christmas.

Knock-knock.
  Who's there?
Rhoda.
  Rhoda who?
Rhoda dendron.

Knock-knock.
  Who's there?
Rich.
  Rich who?
Rich way did he go?

Knock-knock.
  Who's there?
Robin.
  Robin who?
Robin you! Hand over your money!

Knock-knock.
  Who's there?
Roger.
  Roger who?
Roger. Over and out.

Knock-knock.
  Who's there?
Rubber.
  Rubber who?
Rubber the wrong way and she'll smack you.

THISSSSSSS KNOCK-KNOCK BOOK ISSSS SSOMETHING SSSPECIAL!!

Knock-knock.
Who's there?
Safari.
Safari who?
Safari so good.

Knock-knock.
Who's there?
Salome.
Salome who?
Salome on rye with mustard.

Knock-knock.
Who's there?
Sarah.
Sarah who?
Sarah doorbell around here? I'm tired of knocking.

Knock-knock.
Who's there?
Sarasota.
Sarasota who?
Sarasota in the fridge? I'm thirsty.

Knock-knock.
Who's there?
Sari.
Sari who?
Sari, wrong number.

Knock-knock.
Who's there?
Sauna.
Sauna who?
"Sauna clear day you can see forever."

Knock-knock.
Who's there?
Schenectady.
Schenectady who?
Schenectady plug to the socket.

Knock-knock.
Who's there?
Scissors.
Scissors who?
Scissors lovely way to spend the evening.

Knock-knock.
Who's there?
Sedimentary.
Sedimentary who?
Sedimentary, my dear Watson.

Knock-knock.
Who's there?
Serbia.
Serbia who?
Serbia yourself.

Knock-knock.
Who's there?
Sew.
Sew who?
Sew what else is new?

Knock-knock.
Who's there?
Shirley.
Shirley who?
Shirley you know my name.

Knock-knock.
Who's there?
Simmer.
Simmer who?
"Simmer time and the living is easy."

Knock-knock.
Who's there?
Singapore.
Singapore who?
Singapore song or a rich song.

Knock-knock.
Who's there?
Sizzle.
Sizzle who?
Sizzle be my shining hour.

Knock-knock.
Who's there?
Slater.
Slater who?
Slater than you think.

Knock-knock.

Who's there?

Snow.

Snow who?

Snow use using the doorbell, it's broken.

Knock-knock.

Who's there?

Stan.

Stan who?

Stan up and be counted.

Knock-knock.

Who's there?

Stark.

Stark who?

Stark in here, turn on the light.

Knock-knock.
Who's there?
Statue.
Statue who?
Statue in there?

Knock-knock.
Who's there?
Stephen.
Stephen who?
Stephen out with my baby.

Knock-knock.
Who's there?
Stephen.
Stephen who?
Stephen the gas.

Knock-knock.
Who's there?
Stu.
Stu who?
Stu darn hot.

Knock-knock.
Who's there?
Stu.
Stu who?
Stu late now.

Knock-knock.
Who's there?
Tanya.
Tanya who?
Tanya come out and play?

Knock-knock.
Who's there?
Tara.
Tara who?
"Tara-ra-boom-ti-ay."

Knock-knock.
Who's there?
Tarragon.
Tarragon who?
Tarragon with the wind.

82

Knock-knock.
 Who's there?
Tarzan.
 Tarzan who?
Tarzan feather 'em.

Knock-knock.
 Who's there?
Taylor.
 Taylor who?
Taylor I can't make it.

Knock-knock.
 Who's there?
Thayer.
 Thayer who?
Thayer sorry or I'm leaving.

Knock-knock.
 Who's there?
Thee.
 Thee who?
Thee old gray mare.

Knock-knock.
 Who's there?
Theresa.
 Theresa who?
Theresa crowd.

Knock-knock.
Who's there?
Thistle.
Thistle who?
Thistle teach you not to ask silly questions.

Knock-knock.
Who's there?
Tissue.
Tissue who?
Tissue were here.

Knock-knock.
Who's there?
Titus.
Titus who?
Titus a drum.

Knock-knock.
Who's there?
Tobacco.
Tobacco who?
Tobacco your car you have to put it in reverse.

Knock-knock.
Who's there?
Toby.
Toby who?
Toby continued.

Knock-knock.
Who's there?
Tobias.
Tobias who?
Tobias you need a lot of money.

Knock-knock.
Who's there?
Toothache.
Toothache who?
Toothache the high road and I'll take the low road.

Knock-knock.
Who's there?
T. Rex.
T. Rex who?
T. Rex your appetite more than coffee.

Knock-knock.
Who's there?
Turnip.
Turnip who?
Turnip the volume. I can't hear.

Knock-knock.
Who's there?
Twain.
Twain who?
Twain on track nine.

Knock-knock.
Who's there?
Typhoid.
Typhoid who?
Typhoid you were looking for me.

Knock-knock.
  Who's there?
Uma.
  Uma who?
"Uma Darling Clementine."

Knock-knock.
  Who's there?
Upton.
  Upton who?
Upton Sesame.

Knock-knock.
  Who's there?
U-turn.
  U-turn who?
U-turn my legs to jelly.

Knock-knock.
Who's there?
Vanna.
Vanna who?
Vanna go to the movies?

Knock-knock.
Who's there?
Verdi.
Verdi who?
Verdi wave goes, so goes the surfer.

Knock-knock.
Who's there?
Vi.
Vi who?
"Vi do fools fall in love?"

Knock-knock.
Who's there?
Waiter.
Waiter who?
"Waiter till the sun shines, Nellie."

Knock-knock.
Who's there?
Waiver.
Waiver who?
Waiver hands in the air.

Knock-knock.
Who's there?
Wanda.
Wanda who?
Wanda tell me the password? It's cold out here.

Knock-knock.
  Who's there?
Wanda Witch.
  Wanda Witch who?
Wanda Witch you a Merry Christmas.

Knock-knock.
  Who's there?
Weevil.
  Weevil who?
Weevil meet again.

Knock-knock.
  Who's there?
Wiener.
  Wiener who?
Wiener and still champion.

Knock-knock.
  Who's there?
West Point.
  West Point who?
West Point are you trying to make?

Knock-knock.
  Who's there?
Wok.
  Wok who?
Wok, don't run.

Knock-knock.
  Who's there?
Woody.
  Woody who?
Woody want me to say?

Knock-knock.
  Who's there?
Woolly.
  Woolly who?
Woolly win the race?

Knock-knock.
  Who's there?
Wyatt.
  Wyatt who?
Wyatt always pours when it rains?

Knock-knock.
Who's there?
Xena.
Xena who?
Xena picture in the paper.

Knock-knock.
Who's there?
Yale.
Yale who?
"Yale, Caesar."

Knock-knock.
Who's there?
Yawl.
Yawl who?
Yawl come back, you hear.

Knock-knock.
Who's there?
Yoda.
Yoda who?
Yoda smart one, you tell me.

Knock-knock.
Who's there?
Yoga.
Yoga who?
Yoga your way, I'll go mine.

Knock-knock.
Who's there?
Your sister.
Your sister who?
You mean you don't know me?

Knock-knock.
Who's there?
Yukon.
Yukon who?
Yukon win 'em all.

Knock-knock.
Who's there?
Zachery.
Zachery who?
Zachery what I want for Christmas.

Knock-knock.
Who's there?
Zeal.
Zeal who?
Zeal it with a kiss.

Knock-knock.
Who's there?
Zest.
Zest who?
Zest things in life are free.

Knock-knock.
Who's there?
Zinc.
Zinc who?
Zinc like the Titanic.

Knock-knock.
Who's there?
Zoophyte.
Zoophyte who?
Zoophyte anyone who bothers the animals.

Knock-knock.
Who's there?
Zymosis.
Zymosis who?
Zymosis come back with the Ten Commandments?

Knock-knock.
Who's there?
Zone.
Zone who?
Zone worst enemy.

Index